Singing the Journey

SINGING the JOURNEY

A Supplement to
Singing the Living Tradition

UNITARIAN UNIVERSALIST ASSOCIATION
BOSTON

Unitarian Universalist Association
25 Beacon Street
Boston, Massachusetts 02108

Printed on recycled paper
ISBN 1-55896-499-1

10 9 8 7 6 5 4 3 2 1
09 08 07 06 05

Note: Supplemental material related to this publication, including background on contributors, audio files of music, and more, can be found on the UUA's website at www.uua.org/publications.music

The symbol ⊕ indicates that the person named is a Unitarian Universalist.

Dedicated to those exemplars and pioneers
who have pushed the boundaries of congregational music
forward and made this resource possible and necessary.

Contents

JEWISH AND CHRISTIAN TEACHINGS

HUMANIST TEACHINGS

EARTH-CENTERED TRADITIONS

INDEXES

Foreword

Something amazing has happened over the last decade. I've seen congregation after congregation singing hymns without reading from the hymnal, hymns like "Spirit of Life," "Come, Come, Whoever You Are," "We'll Build a Land," and "Gather the Spirit." These and a few others have come to shape our worship and give voice to our theology as we move into this new century. All of these hymns were introduced to most of our congregations when *Singing the Living Tradition*, our current hymnal, was first printed in 1993. We want more people to sing in celebration, in shared community, in despair and in praise, for through song we worship and move the spirit.

And so a dozen years after *Singing the Living Tradition* was published, it is my great pleasure to introduce this new resource for congregational worship.

Singing in community has been central to worship in our tradition for thousands of years. Some of the earliest recorded "hymns" we now know as the Psalms of the Hebrew Bible. Song allows us to name the Holy, to give thanks, to acknowledge both joys and sorrows. We praise, lament, ask for support, and commit ourselves to making justice through song. Singing helps our very "heady" faith find its loving heart. Singing in community brings us together and lets us know that we can raise a clear and unified voice. And we know that a congregation that loves to sing is almost always a vital and strong religious community.

Our music can bind our very individualistic communities together. We struggle to define our shared faith. For many of us it is hard to say simply what Unitarian Universalism is. But the elements of worship that we share help tell us who we are as a religious people. Our songs let us know that we are one religious people despite the many spiritual paths we follow.

Much has changed since 1993, when *Singing the Living Tradition* was introduced. Our congregations have grown in numbers and in membership. Our public witness has led us in from the margins toward the center of the conversation in the public square. And music has become (or is becoming) more central to our life in community. Unitarian Universalist musicians have been composing new hymns that can nurture our spirits now and in years to come. The publication of this music resource offers a selection of these new works to our worshiping community.

In this small volume, you will find hymns that reflect our theological diversity and our respect for the variety of cultural expression. You will also find some new musical vocabularies and new rhythms. But a common thread binds these songs together. These hymns touch the heart as well as the head. They express a Unitarian Universalism that lives and ministers in this complicated world where freedom, peace, and justice are so hard to create and sustain.

Our congregations are large and small, with professional music leadership and without. To make these musical resources more accessible to all of our congregations, we are providing a companion website (see www.uua.org/publications/music) that offers not only more information about the composers and compositions included but also samples of these pieces so that those who help lead the musical lives of our congregations can teach this music more effectively.

A group of extraordinary Unitarian Universalist musicians has worked long and hard to assemble this book. Led by Barbara Wagner, the group includes Leon Burke, Jeannie Gagné, Rev. Dennis Hamilton, Kenneth Herman, and Rev. Jason Shelton. These dedicated and talented professional worship leaders have met and sung each of the more than 1,500 submissions they received to select the pieces you see in this book. I know you will join me in thanks for their labor and their love of this faith. I also want to thank the Unitarian Universalist Musicians Network for their solid support of this new resource. And my personal thanks go to Deborah Weiner, the UUA staff liaison for this project, and to Alison Valentín Chase and Melodie Feather, who provided staff support to help this resource come to fruition.

My hope is that our congregations will find in this book music that will shape our community and give new voice to our values as we move forward, supporting our deepening faith and a more effective voice for justice. And I trust that we will come to love these hymns, and in time, to sing them passionately without looking at this book.

In faith,
Rev. William Sinkford
President, Unitarian Universalist Association

Preface

As you leaf through these pages, you'll find fresh hymns, chants, and songs for marking the seasons of our lives within a myriad of musical styles. We believe that these pieces will encourage your laughter, tears, comfort, and commitment to justice along with a deep sense of compassion and gratitude for all that contributes to our free faith. Our denomination is vibrant, joyful, and thriving — and the music between these covers reflects this amazing good news.

UUA President William G. Sinkford appointed us to the New Hymn Resource Task Force in September of 2003, and we immediately began conversations around the needs for this volume. We solicited submissions through the Unitarian Universalist Musicians Network newsletter, the Unitarian Universalist Ministers Association newsletter, and notices in the UU World and on the UUA website. Simultaneously we researched other hymnals and resources to find music that would enliven UU worship. The result of this far-ranging search was more than 1,500 submissions to the Task Force. We sang through every single one during the course of three face-to-face meetings, striving to find the songs that would bring energy and deep meaning to our worship and our work as Unitarian Universalists.

The charge to choose no more than seventy-five songs was a challenge, but ultimately, we were able to arrive at a collection of wonderful songs and hymns. Just as *Singing the Living Tradition* was guided by the UU Principles and Sources, so this volume is also guided in its content and structure by the six Sources of our living tradition. Three concise indices will help you find your way through the labyrinth of unity and diversity that is *Singing the Journey*.

We are eternally grateful to Lois Allen, our typesetter extraordinaire, and to our gifted and hardworking colleagues who composed, arranged, edited, researched, and tested for us. They gave us comfort and strength, and they gave this project wings. We also gratefully thank the dedicated members of the Unitarian Universalist Musicians Network, who enthusiastically supported this project and have embraced its birth with such joy.

Additional thanks are extended to those who read, reviewed, and helped shape this book. They include Lynn Angebranndt, Thomas Benjamin, Elizabeth Norton, and Catherine Roma.

We were blessed by the challenge and hope offered to us by and through this project, and we are honored by the Unitarian Universalist Association's

faith in us. We hope that you will open your hearts to the extraordinary pos-
sibilities found in this book and sing as though your lives depend upon it.
We bid you to go forward in faith and welcome the messages of these songs
into your souls.

The New Hymns Resource Task Force
Leon Burke
Jeannie Gagné
Dennis Hamilton
Kenneth Herman
Jason Shelton
Barbara Wagner, Chair
Deborah Weiner, Staff Liaison

Singing the Journey

WE, THE MEMBER CONGREGATIONS OF THE
UNITARIAN UNIVERSALIST ASSOCIATION,
COVENANT TO AFFIRM AND PROMOTE:

The inherent worth and dignity of every person;
Justice, equity, and compassion in human relations;
Acceptance of one another and encouragement to spiritual growth
in our congregations;
A free and responsible search for truth and meaning;
The right of conscience and the use of the democratic process
within our congregations and in society at large;
The goal of world community with peace, liberty,
and justice for all;
Respect for the interdependent web of all existence
of which we are a part.

THE LIVING TRADITION WE SHARE DRAWS
FROM MANY SOURCES:

Direct experience of that transcending mystery and wonder,
affirmed in all cultures, which moves us to a renewal of the spirit
and an openness to the forces that create and uphold life;
Words and deeds of prophetic women and men which challenge us
to confront powers and structures of evil with justice, compassion,
and the transforming power of love;
Wisdom from the world's religions which inspire us
in our ethical and spiritual life;
Jewish and Christian teachings which call us to respond to God's love
by loving our neighbors as ourselves;
Humanist teachings which counsel us to heed the guidance of reason
and the results of science, and warn us against
idolatries of the mind and spirit.
Spiritual teachings of Earth-centered traditions which celebrate
the sacred circle of life and instruct us to live in harmony
with the rhythms of nature.

Grateful for the religious pluralism which enriches and ennobles our faith,
we are inspired to deepen our understanding and expand our vision. As free
congregations we enter into this covenant, promising to one another our
mutual trust and support.

The Unitarian Universalist Association shall devote its resources to and exercise its corporate powers for religious, educational, and humanitarian purposes. The primary purpose of the Association is to serve the needs of its member congregations, organize new congregations, extend and strengthen Unitarian Universalist institutions, and implement its principles.

Adopted as a Bylaw by the 1984, 1985, and 1995 General Assemblies.

Morning Has Come

♩ = 112

Use djembe, shaker, drum set, etc. for 12/8 (triplet) groove

1. Morn- ing has come, a - rise and greet the
2. A new day dawns, once more the gift is
3. O - pen our eyes to see that life a -

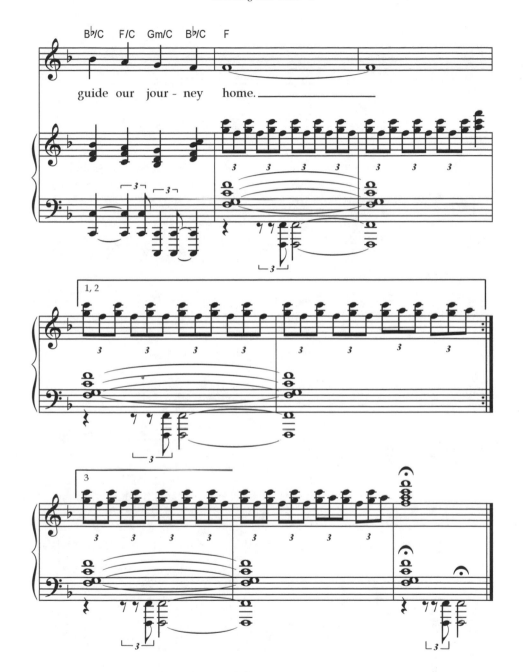

guide our jour - ney home._____

1001   Breaths

Note: *Lower voices may sing piano bass on: dum, da, da, dum, dum, dum.*

Words: Adapted from poem by Birago Diop, 1906 – 1989
⊕ Music: Ysaye M. Barnwell, 1946 – , © 1980 Barnwell's Notes Publishing
(BMI). Used by permission.

An - ces - tor's breath when the fire's ___ voice ___ is heard, 'tis the

An - ces - tor's breath in the voice of the wa - ters. Zah

To Coda Last Time

Whsshh Aahh Whsshh

1. Those who have
2. Those who have

grass,   they are   in   the moan - ing   rocks.   The
homes,   they are with   us in   this   crowd.   The

dead are   not   un - der the   earth._____   So
dead have   a   pact with the   liv - ing._____   So

Repeat ad lib. and dim. Fermata is only used on the last repeat.

Whsshh   Aahh   Whsshh   Zah_____

1002 Comfort Me

3. Speak for me. . .   4. Dance with me. . .   5. Comfort me. . .

Where Do We Come From?   1003

Where do we come from? What are we? Where are we go-ing?

Where   do   we   come   from?

Mys-te-ry.   Mys-te-ry.   Life is a rid-dle and a mys-te-ry.

Where__ do we come from? Where__ are we go-ing?

Words: Paul Gaugin, 1848 – 1903 and Brian Tate, 1954 – , © 1999 Brian Tate
Music: Brian Tate, 1954 – , © 1999 Brian Tate

1004

Busca el Amor

1. Re - vi - sa tu cor - a - zón__ Pa - ra ha - llar el a -
2. Re - gi - stra tu ca - ma - león__ Cuan - do cam - bia el co -

mor en un rin - cón_____ Pe - ro bus - ca el a - mor Ni pla - cer
lor del cor - a - zón_____ Y te es - ta - lla la flor Un pé - ta -

Words & music: Salvador Cardenal Barquero, 1960 – , © 1999 Salvador Cardenal Barquero,
⊕ arr. Jason Shelton, 1972 –
English trans. Ted Warmbrand, 1943 – , and Jacqueline Schwartz Turchick, 1942 –

1. Examine that heart of yours
   As you look for the love on
   your high shelf
   Past the pleasure and passion
   for your own self
   For the love that's reaching
   someone else.

2. Your heart's a chameleon
   Ever open to change
   like any flower
   Spreading out for the sun,
   petals bursting with power
   To be love that's reaching
   someone else.

1005　Praise in Springtime

1. Praise to God and thanks we bring, hearts re-joice and__ voic-es sing; prais-es to the Glo-rious One; for a year of won-der done. Praise now for the
2. Praise now for the sum-mer rain; feed-ing day and__ night with grain; praise now for the ti-ny seed; hold-ing all the word shall need; Praise now for the
3. Praise now for the snow-y rest, fal-ling soft on__ na-ture's breast; for the hap-py dreams of birth, brood-ing in the qui-et earth. For this year of

⊕ Words: William Channing Gannett, 1840 – 1923
⊕ Music: Thomas Benjamin, 1940 – , © 1990 Thomas Benjamin

1006   In My Quiet Sorrow

1. I am worn, I am tired,
2. I won't speak of this ache
3. I keep on, day by day,
4. You're my hope when I fear

in my qui - et sor - row.
in - side, light e - ludes me.
trust - ing light will guide me.
hold - ing on, be - liev - ing.

⊕Words & music: Jeannie Gagné, 1960 – , © 2004 Jeannie Gagné

1007   There's a River Flowin' in My Soul

Slow gospel feel ♩ = 120

There's a — riv-er —— flow-in' in my heart. —
soul. —
mind. —

There's a riv-er —— flow-in' in my heart. —
soul. —
mind. —

And it's tell - in' me that I'm some - bo - dy —

Words & music: Rose Sanders, 1945 – ,
arr. Kenny Smith, 1965 –

1008   When Our Heart Is in a Holy Place

⊕ Words & music: Joyce Poley, 1941 – , © 1996 Songstyle Music (SOCAN),
keyboard arr. Lorne Kellett, 1950 –

Meditation on Breathing   1009

⊕Words & music: Sarah Dan Jones, 1962 – , © 2001 Sarah Dan Jones

1010   We Give Thanks

⊕ Words & music: Wendy Luella Perkins, 1966 – , © 2004 Wendy Luella Perkins,
⊕ arr. Susan Peck, 1960 –

Return Again

1011

Re-turn a - gain, Re - turn a - gain,____ Re -
turn to the home of your soul,____ soul.____

Re-turn to who you are, Re - turn to what you are,
Re - turn to where you are born and re - born a-gain.

1012   When I Am Frightened

1. When I am fright-ened, will you re-as-sure me?
2. When I am an-gry, will you still em-brace me?
3. When I am troub-led, will you lis-ten to me?

When I'm un-cer-tain, will you hold my hand?
When I am thought-less, will you un-der-stand?
When I am lone-ly, will you be my friend?

⊕ Words & music: Shelley Jackson Denham, 1950 – , © 1999 Shelley Jackson Denham,
⊕ arr. Jeannie Gagné, 1960 –
    ETHICAL RELATIONS, Irregular

— then I may learn to care as you
— then I may learn to give as you
— then I may learn to love as you

do, then I may learn to care.
do, then I may learn to give.
do, then I may learn to

love. _____

Open My Heart

1013

Open my heart to all that I seek; Let me be part of the Love You give.

1014   Standing on the Side of Love

Moderate rock feel, with passion and dignity ♩= 72

1. The prom - ise of the Spir - it:___
2. Some - times we build a bar - rier___
3. A bright new day is dawn - ing___

⊕ Words & music: Jason Shelton, 1972 – , © 2004 Yelton Rhodes Music (ASCAP).
Used by permission.
SINKFORD, 7.6.5.5.8 with refrain

1015   I Know I Can

⊕ Words: Dennis Hamilton, 1944 –
⊕ Music: Jeannie Gagné, 1960 –,
⊕ arr. Mark Freundt, 1966 –

3. My sister in my heart,
   My brother in my song,
   Though troubles wait at every turn,
   I know I can go on.

4. And though the journey is long,
   The destination is near,
   Though troubles wait at every turn,
   I know I can go on.

5. So brothers take my hand
   And sisters sing my song,
   When hope awaits at every turn,
   I know we will go on.

1016 Profetiza, Pueblo Mío
(Prophesy, Oh My People)

Pro - fe - ti - za, Pue-blo mí - o, pro-fe-ti-za u-na vez
Proph-e - sy, _____ oh my peo - ple, proph-e - sy_____ one more

más. Que tu voz sea al e - co del cla-mor de los
time. Let your voice_____ be the ech - o of the

Pue - blos en o - pre - sión. Pro - fe - ti - za, Pue - blo
out - cries of all op - pressed. Proph-e - sy, _____ oh my

mí - o, pro-fe - ti-za u-na vez más, a - nun-
peo - ple, proph-e - sy_____ one more time. An -

Words & music: Rosa Martha Zárate Macias © 1989 Rosa Martha Zárate Macias,
⊕ arr. Kenneth Herman, 1944 -
⊕ English trans. Elsie Zala, 1925 -

cían - do - le_a los po - bres u - na nue - va so - cie -
nounce to them the com - ing of a new so - ci - e -

dad. 1. Pro - fe - ta te con - sa - gro,_____
ty. 1. I sanc - ti - fy you, proph - et._____

Fine *Stanzas*

no_ha - ya du - da_y te - mor en tu_an - dar por la_his -
Ban - ish all doubt and fear. Be faith - ful to your

to - ria;_____ sé fiel a tu mi - sión.
mis - sion;_____ the quest that leads us on.

To refrain

2. Anúnciales‿a los Pueblos
   que se renovará
   el pacto‿en la justicia:
   la paz florecerá.

3. Denuncia‿a quienes causan
   el llanto‿y la‿opresión
   la verdad sea tu‿escudo
   sé luz de‿un nuevo sol.

4. Esta sea tu‿esperanza,
   este sea tu luchar,
   construir‿en la justicia
   la nueva sociedad.

2. *Announce to all the people*
   that justice promised long,
   Restored to every nation;
   true peace throughout the world.

3. *Denounce all who are causing*
   oppression, sorrow, tears,
   Let truth be your protection,
   the light of a new sun.

4. *Let this be what you hope for,*
   the battle that you choose:
   To build a social order
   with justice at its core.

1017 Building a New Way

Words & music: Martha Sandefer, 1952 – , © 1986 Martha Sandefer,
⊕ arr. Jim Scott, 1946 –

3. We can feed our every need (3X)
   Start with love, that is the seed.
   We can feed our every need.

4. Peace and freedom is our cry (3X)
   Without these this world will die.
   Peace and freedom is our cry.

1018   Come and Go with Me

Words & music: African-American spiritual, slavery period,
arr. Kenny Smith, 1965 –

3. There'll be justice in that land. . .
4. There'll be singin' in that land. . .

1019　　Everything Possible

✣ Words & music: Fred Small, 1952 – , © 1983 Pine Barrens Music (BMI),
arr. Willi Zwozdesky, 1955 – , © 2004 Willi Zwozdesky
(SOCAN) Rhythmic Trident Music Publishing. Used by permission.

1020

Woyaya

Words & music: Loughty Amoa, Solomon Amarfio, Robert M. Bailey, Roy Bedeau,
Francis T. Osei, Whendell K. Richardson, and Mac Tontoh © Chappell & Co., Inc.
All rights reserved. Used by permission. Warner Bros. Publications US, Inc., Miami, FL 33014
⊕ Transcribed from Ysaye M. Barnwell, 1946 - ,
⊕ arr. Jeannie Gagné, 1960 -

1021   Lean on Me

1. Some-times in our lives____ we all have pain,____ we all have sor - row.____
2. Please swal-low your pride____ if I have things. you need to bor - row,____
3. If there is a load____ you have to bear____ that you can't car - ry,____

But if we are wise____ we know that there's.
For no one can fill____ those of your needs.
I'm right up the road,____ I'll share your load____

you need a hand.__ We all__ need some-bod-y to lean_

_____ on. I just might have a prob-lem that

you'd un-der-stand.__ We all__ need some-bod-y to lean____ on.__

1022 Open the Window

⊕ Words & music: Elise Witt, 1953– , inspired by the Georgia Sea Islands spiritual
"Heist the Window, Noah," © 1997 Elise Witt (ASCAP) and © 1997 Non Si Sa Mai Music (ASCAP),
⊕ keyboard arr. Jeannie Gagné, 1960–

4. Some people have money, some people have none.
   What's the use of money if your heart's gone numb?

5. This big old world is in a great big mess.
   Open the window find peace and rest.

O - pen___ the win-dow let the dove fly___ in. Ba -
Don't
The

- by is a cry - in' like her heart___ will break___
see what's to dis - cov - er on the oth - er side.___
on - ly bor - der close you is the bor - der 'round your mind.

O - pen___ the win-dow let the dove fly___ in.

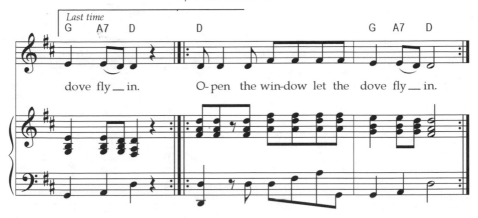

dove fly — in.   O- pen the win-dow let the   dove fly — in.

Building Bridges   1023

Build - ing Bridg-es — be - tween   our di - vi - sions, —   I

reach   out to you,   will you reach   out   to me?   With

all   of our voic-es — and all   of our vi-sions,

friends, we could make such   sweet   har-mo-ny.

Words: The women of Greenham Common peace occupation in England, 1983
Music: Contemporary English Quaker Round

1024　When the Spirit Says Do

*Note: Replace "do" with other words: sing, dance, laugh, shout, etc.
Return to "do" for last time.*

Words & music: African–American spiritual, civil rights period,
⊕ arr. Mark Freundt, 1966 –

When Will the Fighting Cease?

1025

Translation of Latin: Give peace, Lord, in our time.

⊕ Words: Nick Page, 1952– and ⊕ Nita Penfold, 1950– , © 2002 Nick Page
Music: Melchior Franck, c. 1579–1639

1026   If Every Woman in the World

Gospel waltz

1. If ev'-ry   wom-an___ in the   world___ had her
(2. If ev'-ry) man_____ in the   world___ had his
(3. If ev'-ry) lead - er___ in the   world___ shared a
(4. If ev'-ry) na - tion   in the   world___ set   a

mind set   on___ free - dom, if ev'-ry   wom-an___ in the
mind set   on___ free - dom, if ev'-ry   broth-er___ stood with
vi - sion   of___ free - dom, if ev'-ry   lead - er___ in the
true course for___ free - dom, if ev'-ry   na - tion___ raised its

Words: Karen MacKay (verse 1), 1952 – ; Nancy L. Nordlie (verses 2-4), 1953 –
Music: Karen MacKay, 1952 – , © 1984 Karen MacKay,
arr. Jerome Kyles, 1974 – ; ed. by Nancy L. Nordlie, 1953 –

Cuando el Pobre

(When the Poor Ones)

1027

♩. = 80

1. Cuan-do_el po - bre_____ na - da tie - ne_____ y_aún re -
1. When the poor ones,____ who have noth - ing,____ still are

par-te,_____ cuan-do al - guien_ pa - sa
giv - ing;_____ when the thirst - y_ pass the

sed y_a-gua nos da, cuan-do_el
cup, wa - ter to share; when the

dé - bil_____ a su_her-ma-no_____ for - ta - le - ce,_____
wound-ed_____ of - fer oth - ers strength and heal-ing:_____

Words: Spanish - Jose Antonio Oliver, 1939- ; English - Martin A. Seltz, 1951–
Music: Jose Antonio Olivar and Miquel Manzano, © 1971, Jose Antonio Olivar and
Miguel Manzano. Published by OCP Publicaitons, 5536 NE Hassalo, Portland, OR 97213.
All rights reserved. Used with permission.
Arr. Alvin Schutmaat.
EL CAMINO, 12.11.12.11.11

2. Cuando‿alguno sufre‿y logra su consuelo,
   cuando‿espera‿y no se cansa de‿esperar,
   cuando‿amamos, aunque‿el odio nos rodee,
   va Dios mismo‿en nuestro mismo caminar;
   va Dios mismo‿en nuestro mismo caminar.

2. *When compassion gives the suff'ring consolation;*
   when expecting brings to birth hope that was lost;
   when we choose love, not the hatred all around us:
   we see God, here by our side, walking our way,
   we see God, here by our side, walking our way.

3. Cuando crece la‿alegría‿y nos inunda,
   cuando dicen nuestros labios la verdad,
   cuando‿añoramos el sentir de los sencillos,
   va Dios mismo‿en nuestro mismo caminar;
   va Dios mismo‿en nuestro mismo caminar.

> 3. *When our spirits, like a chalice, brim with gladness;*
> *when our voices, full and clear, sing out the truth;*
> *when our longings, free from envy, seek the humble:*
> *we see God, here by our side, walking our way,*
> *we see God, here by our side, walking our way.*

4. Cuando‿abunda‿el bien y llena los hogares,
   cuando‿alguien donde‿hay guerra pone paz,
   cuando‿"hermano" le llamamos al extraño
   va Dios mismo‿en nuestro mismo caminar;
   va Dios mismo‿en nuestro mismo caminar.

> 4. *When the goodness poured from heaven fills our dwellings;*
> *when the nations work to change war into peace;*
> *when the stranger is accepted as our neighbor:*
> *we see God, here by our side, walking our way,*
> *we see God, here by our side, walking our way.*

1028 The Fire of Commitment

1. From the light of days re - mem - bered burns a
(2. From the) stor - ies of our liv - ing rings a
(3. From the) dreams of youth - ful vis - ion comes a

bea - con bright and clear   Guid - ing hands and hearts and
song both brave and free   Call - ing pil - grims still to
new, pro - phet - ic voice   Which de - mands a deep - er

Note: The use of percussion is highly recommended.

⊕ Words: Mary Katherine Morn, 1961 – and Jason Shelton, 1972 –
⊕ Music: Jason Shelton, 1972 –, © 2001 Jason Shelton
FIRE OF COMMITMENT, 8.7.8.7 with refrain

Love Knocks and Waits for Us to Hear   1029

1. Love knocks and waits for us to hear, to
2. Love of-fers life, in spite of foes who
3. Love comes to heal the bro-ken heart, to
4. Love knocks and en - ters at the sound of

o - pen and in - vite; Love longs to qui - et
threat-en and con - demn; em - brac-ing en - e -
ease the troub - led mind; with - out a word Love
wel-come from with - in; Love sings and danc - es

eve - ry fear, and seeks to set things right.
mies, Love goes the sec - ond mile with them.
bids us start to ask and seek and find.
all a - round, and feels new life be - gin.

Words & music: Daniel Charles Damon, 1955 – , © 1996 Hope Publishing Co.,
Carol Stream, IL 60188. All rights reserved. Used by permission.
ANGEL'S CAMP, C.M.

1030

Siyahamba
(We Are Marching)

Note: Replace "marching" with other words: singing, dancing, walking, etc.

Words & music: South Africa, 20th Cent.
ed. Anders Nyberg, © 1984 Utryck. Walton Music Corp. admin. Used by permission.
SIYAHAMBA, Irregular

Spanish: Caminando en la luz de Dios (4X)
(Melody)   Caminando
(Harmony)   Caminando, vamos Caminando, vamos
(Both)   Caminando en la luz de Dios.

Filled with Loving Kindness   1031

*Note: Second time: Replace each "I" with "you."
Third time: Replace each "I" with "we."

Words: Traditional Buddhist Meditation;
⊕ adapted by Mark W. Hayes, 1949 – , © 2001 Mark W. Hayes
⊕ Music: Ian W. Riddell, 1968 – , © 2001 Ian W. Riddell

1032

Daoona Nayeesh

Da-oo-na na-yeesh bee - sa - laam___

da-oo - na na - yeesh Bee - a - maan

da-oo - na nan - sij

*Translation from Arabic: Let us live in peace. Let us live in inner peace.
Let us weave our dreams together. Let us die in peace.*

Words: Samir Badri, 1952 –
    Music: Ted Warmbrand, 1943 – , © 2002 Ted Warmbrand,
⊕ arr. Jeannie Gagné, 1960 –

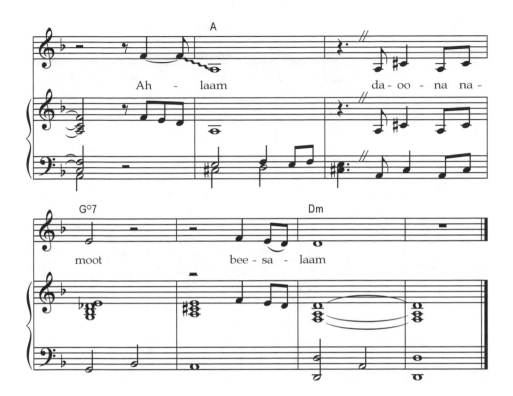

Ah - laam   da - oo - na na -

moot   bee - sa - laam

1033

Bwana Awabariki

Bwa - na a-wa-ba-ri - ki, Bwa - na a-wa-ba-ri - ki,
May God grant you a bless-ing, may God grant you a bless-ing,

Bwa - na a-wa-ba-ri - ki, mi - le - le.
may God grant you a bless-ing ev - er - more.

*U - ki-mcha Bwa - na. Bwa - na a - wa - ba - ri - ki.
Re-vere the Lord. May God grant you a bless - ing.

*Note: Insert personal words: i.e.
"Thanks to our teachers"
"Peace to all nations"*

Words: Swahili folk hymn
Music: Swahili melody

De Noche

Note: *The Taizé songs are meant to be sung with numerous repetitions and in whichever language you choose.*

French: De nuit nous irons dans l'ombre, car pour découvrir la source, seule la soif nous éclaire.

Italian: Di notte andremo, di notte, per incontrare la fonte, solo la sete c'illumina, solo la sete ci guida.

German: In Dunkler Nacht woll'n wir ziehen, lebendiges Wasser finden. Nur unser Durst wird uns leuchten, nur unser Durst wird uns leuchten.

Words: Unknown
Music: Jacques Berthier, 1923 – 1994, © Les Presses de Taizé (France).

1035   Freedom Is Coming

Words & music: South African, 20th Cent.

Calypso Alleluia

1036

Gently swung, with a Calypso or Latin feeling ♩ = 132

Al - le-lu - ia, sing_ al - le - lu - ia! ___ Sing_
Bles - sed be, ___ sing_ bles - sed be! ___ Sing_

Al - le-lu - i-a, al - le-lu - i-a, al - le - lu - ia. Sing_
Bles-sed, bles-sed be, bles-sed, bles-sed be, bles - sed be. ___ Sing_

Al - le - lu - ia, sing al - le - lu - ia!
Bles - sed_ be, ___ sing bles - sed_ be.

Low Drum

Claves

Shaker

Note: This should be sung if possible with Latin percussion.
It may be performed by layering or as a round.
The fermata is observed only at the end.
Other phrases may be substituted for the given texts.

⊕ Words & music: Thomas Benjamin, 1940 – , © 2004 Thomas Benjamin

1037   We Begin Again in Love

Narrator: For remaining silent when a single voice would have made a difference. . .

(Congregation sings each time in response: "We forgive ourselves and each other. We begin again in love.")

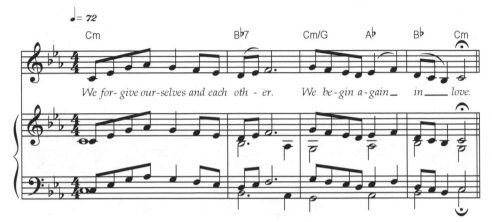

For each time that our fears have made us rigid and inaccessible. . .

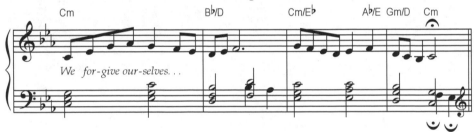

For each time we have struck out in anger without just cause. . .

⊕ Words: Robert Eller-Isaacs, 1951 –
⊕ Music: Les Kleen, 1942 – , © 1996 Les Kleen

For each time that our greed has blinded us to the needs of others. . .

For the selfishness that set us apart and alone. . .

For falling short of the admonitions of the spirit. . .

For losing sight of our unity. . .

For those and for so many acts both evident and subtle which have fueled the illusion of separateness. . .

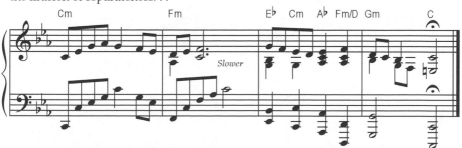

1038

The 23rd Psalm
Dedicated to My Mother

1. The Lord is my shepherd, I have all I need,
2. Even though I walk through a dark and drear-y land
3. Surely, surely goodness and kindness will follow me all the days of my life,

She makes me lie down in green meadows. Beside the still wa-ters, She will lead.
There is nothing that can shake me, She has said She won't forsake me, I'm in her hand.
And I will live in Her house, forever, for-ev-er and ev-er.

She restores my soul, She rights my wrongs,
She sets a table before me in the pre-sence of my foes,
Glory be to our Mother and Daughter and to the Ho-ly of Ho-lies.

She leads me in the path of good things, She fills my heart with songs.
She anoints my head with oil, and my cup o-ver-flows.
As it was in the beginning, is now and ever shall be world with-out end. A-men.

Words: Adapted from the Book of Psalms by Bobby McFerrin, 1950 –
Music: Bobby McFerrin, 1950 – , © 2003 ProbNoblem Music (BMI),
c/o Original Artists, 826 Broadway, New York, NY 10003. All rights reserved.
Used by permission.

Be Thou with Us

1039

Words: Daniel Budd, 1951 – , © 1994 Daniel Budd
⊕ Music: Thomas Benjamin, 1940 – , © 1995 Thomas Benjamin

1040

Hush

Words & music: African-American spiritual, slavery period,
⊕ arr. Jason Shelton, 1972 -

4. Soon one mornin', death come creepin' in my room . . .

5. I'm so glad trouble don't last always . . .

1041

Santo

Dios. / God.

1. Que a-com-pa ña a nue - stro pue - blo, que
1. Who com - pan - ions all the peo - ple, who
vi - ve en nues - tras - lu - chas, el u - ni - ver - so en -
lives with - in our strug-gles, the u - ni - ver - sal
te - ro, el ú - ni - co Se - ñor.
Sov' - reign, One God lead-ing us on.

2. Benditos los que en su nombre el Evangelio anuncian,
   la buena y gran noticia de la liberación.

2. *Bles-sed are those who, in God's name give witness to the Gospel,*
   the news of liberation, for all peoples of earth.

1042   Rivers of Babylon

Reggae swing ♩ = 132

Note: No pedal.

By the riv-ers of Ba-by-lon_____ there we sat down_____

_____ and there we wept_____ when we re-mem-ber

words of ___ our ___ mouths and ___ the med-i - ta- tion of ___ our ___

hearts be ac - cept-a-ble in Thy sight, O Far-

ai. ___ So let the ai

1043

Székely Áldás
(Székely Blessing)

♩ = 84

Part 1: Hol __ hit ott __ sze-re-tet; hol __ sze-re-tet ott __ bé-ke. Hol __

Part 2: Where __ there is faith there is love; where __ there is love there is peace.

Note: First time: Part 1 only.
      Second time: Part 2 only.
      Third time: both parts together.

Pronunciation Guide:
Hol hit ott sze- re- tet;
Hawl heet, awt seh-reh-teht
hol sze- re- tet ott bé- ke.
Hawl seh-reh-teht, awt bay-keh
Hol bé- ke ott ál- dás;
Hawl bay-keh, awt ahl-dahsh
Hol ál- dás ott I- sten.
Hawl ahl-dahsh awt Eesh-ten
Hol I- sten ott szük- ség nin-csen.
Hawl eesh-ten, awt sewk-shayg neensch-shen.

Words: Traditional Transylvanian
⊕Music: Elizabeth H. Norton, 1959 – , © 2002 Elizabeth H. Norton

1044

Eli, Eli
(Walking to Caesaria)

*Note: "Eli" is pronounced "ay-lee"

Words: Hannah Senesh, 1921 - 1944
Music: David Zehavi, c. 1910 - 1975,
⊕ arr. Kenneth Herman, 1944 -

1045   There Is a Balm in Gilead

Words & music: African-American spiritual, slavery period.
arr. Nolan Williams, Jr. © 2000. Used by permission of
GIA Publications, Inc., 7404 South Mason Ave., Chicago, IL 60638. All rights reserved.

think   my work's   in   vain,   But___   then   the   Ho - ly
can - not   pray   like   Paul,   You can   tell   the   love   of

Spir - it   Re - vives my soul a - gain.___   There___ is a
Je - sus,   And   say "He died for   all!"___   There___ is a

1046 Shall We Gather at the River

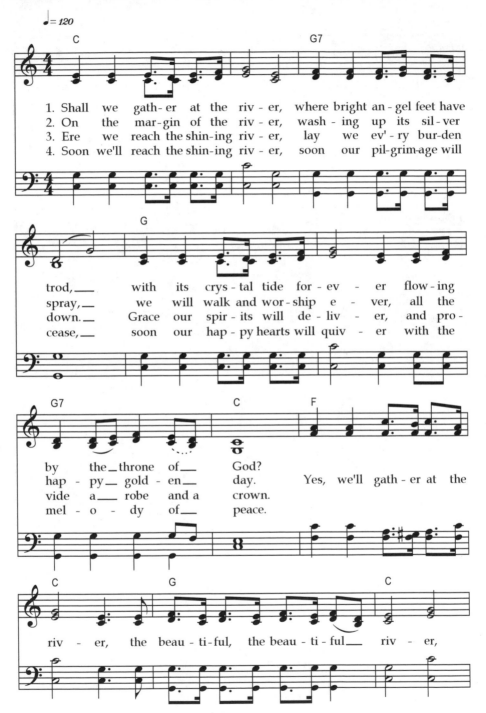

1. Shall we gath-er at the riv-er, where bright an-gel feet have
2. On the mar-gin of the riv-er, wash-ing up its sil-ver
3. Ere we reach the shin-ing riv-er, lay we ev'-ry bur-den
4. Soon we'll reach the shin-ing riv-er, soon our pil-grim-age will

trod,— with its crys-tal tide for-ev-er flow-ing
spray,— we will walk and wor-ship e-ver, all the
down.— Grace our spir-its will de-liv-er, and pro-
cease,— soon our hap-py hearts will quiv-er with the

by the throne of God?
hap-py gold-en day. Yes, we'll gath-er at the
vide a robe and a crown.
mel-o-dy of peace.

riv-er, the beau-ti-ful, the beau-ti-ful riv-er,

Words & music: Robert Lowry, 1826 – 1899; First published in *Happy Voices* in 1865.
HANSON PLACE, 8.7.8.7 with refrain

gath- er with the saints_ at the riv - er that flows by the throne of_God.

Nada Te Turbe

1047

♩= 72

Spanish: Na- da te tur - be, na - da te_es-pan - te
Noth-ing can troub - le, noth-ing can fright - en.

qui_en a Dios tie - ne na-da le fal - ta. Na-da te tur - be,
Those that seek God shall ne-ver go want-ing. Noth-ing can troub - le,

na - da te_es-pan - te Só - lo Dios ba - sta.
noth-ing can fright - en. God a - lone fills us.

Words: Santa Teresa de Jesús
Music: Jacques Berthier, 1923 – 1994, © Les Presses de Taizé (France).

1048 Ubi Caritas

U - bi ca - ri - tas   et a - mor,___
u - bi ca - ri - tas   De - us i - bi est.

Translation of Latin: Where charity and love abound, God is there.

1049 Vieni Spirito Creatore

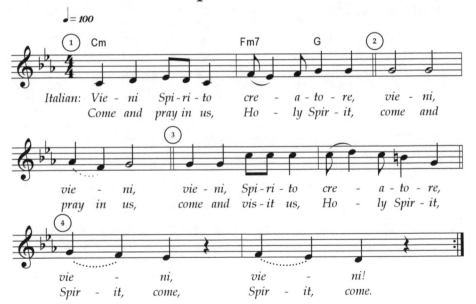

Italian: Vie - ni Spi-ri - to   cre - a - to - re,   vie - ni,
Come and pray in us,   Ho - ly Spir - it,   come and

vie - ni,   vie - ni, Spi - ri - to   cre - a - to - re,
pray in us,   come and vis - it us,   Ho - ly Spir - it,

vie - ni,   vie - ni!
Spir - it, come,   Spir - it, come.

Spanish: Ven Espíritu, fuente de vida. Ven, ven, ven Señor.
Ven Espíritu, fuente de vida. Ven Señor, ven Señor.

Note: The Taizé songs are meant to be sung with numerous repetitions and in whichever language you choose.

Attribution for both *Ubi Caritas* and *Vieni Spirito Creatore*
Words: Unknown
Music: Jacques Berthier, 1923 – 1994, © Les Presses de Taizé (France).
Used by permission of GIA Publications, exclusive agent. All rights reserved.

Jazz Alleluia

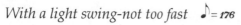

1051

We Are...

Note: Repeat this 4 measure chord pattern throughout the piece.

⊕ Words & music: Ysaye M. Barnwell, 1946 – , © 1991 Barnwell's Notes Publishing (BMI). Used by permission.

grand - fa - thers' dream - ings, we_____ are the

breath of our an - ces - tors, we____ are the spir - it of God. We are

moth - ers of cour - age and fa - thers of time, we are

daugh - ters of dust and the sons of great vi - sions, we're

sis- ters of mer-cy and broth-ers of love, we are

lov-ers of life and the build-ers of na-tions, we're seek-ers of truth and

keep-ers of faith, we are mak-ers of peace and the wis-dom of a - ges.

We are___ our grand-moth-ers' prayers and we___ are our

grand - fa - thers' dream - ings, we____ are the

breath of our an - ces - tors, we____ are the spir - it of God. For

each child that's born, a morn - ing star ri - ses and

| 1, 2, 3 | 4 |

sings to the u - ni - verse who__ we are. For who__ we are.

1052   The Oneness of Everything

1. Far beyond the grasp of hands, or light to meet the eye, past the reach-es of the
2. Peace is in the dance of trees, who stir be-fore the first breath of wind is yet per-
3. Still we seek to find a truth that we might un-der-stand and re-duce to terms de-

⊕ Words & music: Jim Scott, 1946 – , © 2002 Jim Scott

flight tak - ing the weight of the world up - on its
ny gives to us all lives worth liv -
life en - ters my soul as a song_____ to

wings,_____ In the one - ness of ev' - ry -
ing,_____ For the one - ness of ev' - ry -
sing,_____ Of the one - ness of ev' - ry -

Coda after verse 3

thing.
thing.
thing.

1053   How Could Anyone

How could an-y-one ev - er tell you you were an-y-thing less than beau-ti - ful?__ How could an-y-one ev - er tell you__ you were less than

1054 Let This Be a House of Peace

1. Let this be a house of peace
2. Let this be a house of free -
3. Let all in this house seek truth
4. Let this be a house of pro -

- dom;
Of na - ture and hu - man - i - ty, of
Guar - di - an of dig - ni - ty and
Where sci - en - tists and mys - tics a -
- phe-sy May vi - sion, for our chil - dren

⊕ Words: Jim Scott, 1946 – , inspired by Kenneth Patton, 1911 – 1994
⊕ Music: Jim Scott, 1946 – , © 1999 Jim Scott

1055   How Sweet the Darkness

1. When windows that are black and cold are
2. When wings pursue their proper flight and
3. And when the sky is swept of wars and

lit a-new with fires of gold; When
bring not terror but delight; When
keeps but gentle moon and stars, That

dusk in quiet shall descend and
clouds are innocent again and
peaceful sky, that harmless air, how

dark-ness come once more a friend.
hide no storms of deadly rain;
sweet, how sweet, the dark-ness there.

Words: Rachel Bates
⊕ Music: Jason Shelton, 1972 – , © 2002 Jason Shelton
MAURO, L.M.

Pronunciation: Too lah klih zee yo
Nah lah pah sey ky ya
Ey ky ya
Nah lah pah sey ky yah

Translation of Zulu: *Be still my heart, even here I am at home.*

Words & music: Joseph Shabalala, 1941 – ,
⊕ as taught by Nick Page, 1952 – (by rote, a cappella, and with a dance)

1057

Go Lifted Up

Words & music: Mortimer B. Barron, 1939 – , © 1993, 2004 Mortimer Barron

1058   Be Ours a Religion

Be ours a re - li - gion which like sun - shine goes
eve - ry - where, its___ tem - ple all space, its
shrine the good heart, its creed all truth, its

⊕ Words: Theodore Parker, 1810 – 1860
⊕ Music: Thomas Benjamin, 1940 – , © 1998 Yelton Rhodes Music (ASCAP). Used by permission.

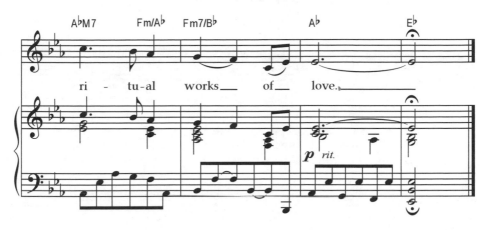

ri – tu-al works___ of___ love.___

May Your Life Be As a Song   1059

♩ = *140*

1 May your life be as a song, Re –

2 sound-ing with the dawn to sing a-wake the light. And

3 soft – ly se – re – nade the stars, Ev – er

4 danc – ing cir – cles in the night.

⊕ Words: Jim Scott, 1946 –
  Music: Yuri Zaritsky

1060   As We Sing of Hope and Joy

1. As we sing of___ hope and joy to - day,
2. If a crum - bling world we would re - new,
3. Let this song our___ great - est hopes con - tain:
4. Sing of joy while___ ham - mer - ing each nail.

Some know on - ly___ an - guish and des - pair.
We must sing no___ or - di - nar - y song,
Laugh - ter of a___ well - fed child its tune,
Sing of hope while___ pull - ing eve - ry weed,

How can we lift our voic - es in this way while
Peals from a nois - y gong will ne - ver do; in
Roofs o - ver eve - ry heart - beat its re - frain, its
So shall we sing to - geth - er and pre - vail; May

⊕ Words & music: Elizabeth Alexander, 1962 – , © 1995, 2004 Elizabeth Alexander

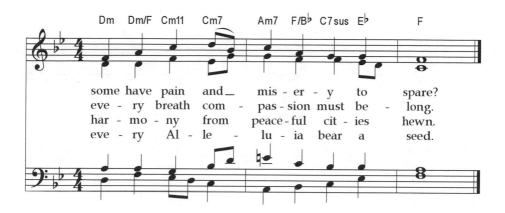

some have pain and_ mis - er - y to spare?
eve - ry breath com - pas - sion must be - long.
har - mo - ny from peace - ful cit - ies hewn.
eve - ry Al - le - lu - ia bear a seed.

1061 For So the Children Come

Gently ♩= 72

Each night a child is born is a ho-ly night: A time for sing-ing, A time for won-der-ing, A time for wor-ship-ping, Each night a child is born is a ho-ly night. (ho-ly night)

⊕ Words: Sophia Lyon Fahs, 1876 – 1978
⊕ Music: Jason Shelton, 1972 – , © 1998 Jason Shelton

(Narrator)
1. For so the children come
   And so they have been coming
   Always the same way they come
   Born of the seed of a man and a woman.

(Congregation sings)   *Each night a child . . .*

(Narrator)
2. No angels herald their beginnings
   No prophets predict their future courses
   No wise men see a star to show where to find
   The babe that will save humankind

(Congregation)   *Each night a child . . .*

(Narrator)
3. Yet each night a child is born is a holy night
   Fathers and mothers - sitting beside their children's cribs
   Feel glory in the sight of new life beginning
   They ask, "Where and how will this new life end?
   Or will it ever end?"

(Congregation)   *Each night a child . . .*

(Narrator)
4. Each night a child is born is a holy night -
   A time for singing
   A time for wondering
   A time for worshipping

(Congregation)   *Each night a child . . .*

1062   All Around the Child

In traditional carol style ♩= 92

1. An - cient sto - ry___ lived a - gain,___
2. New life fra - gile___ yet com - plete,___
3. May our won - der___ ne - ver cease,___
4. Vi - sion for hu - man - i - ty,___

dark of long - est___ night.
life from love___ once___ more.
Na - ture's great - est___ art.
all a - round___ the___ child.

⊕ Words & music: Jim Scott, 1946 – , © 2002 Jim Scott

Winter Solstice Chant

1063

⊕ Words & music: Phillip Palmer, 1980 – , © 2003 Phillip Palmer,
⊕ arr. Jeannie Gagné, 1960 –

1064

Blue Boat Home

Fluid, legato ♩ = *140*

1. Though be - low me, I feel no mo - tion
2. Sun my sail___ and moon my rud - der
3. I give thanks to the waves up - hold - ing me,

⊕ Words: Peter Mayer, 1963 – , © 2002 Peter Mayer
   Music: Roland Hugh Prichard, 1811 – 1887, adapted by Peter Mayer, 1963 – ,
      © 2002 Peter Mayer,
⊕ keyboard arr. Jason Shelton, 1972 –
      HYFRODOL, 8.7.8.7.D

stan-ding on these moun-tains and plains.
as I ply the star - ry sea,
hail the great winds urg - ing me on,

Far a - way from the rol - ling o - cean
lean - ing o - ver the edge in won - der,
greet the in - fi - nite sea be - fore__ me,

still my dry land heart__ can say:
cast - ing ques - tions in - to the deep.
sing the sky my sai - lor's song:

1065

Alabanza

(As the Rain Is Falling)

♩ = 92

Em   **Am7**   **B**

1. Al ca - er la llu - via re - sur - ge con ver -
2. El 'co - quí' se a - le - gra, se sien - te muy fe -
1. As the rain is fall - ing, the for - est is re -
2. The 'co - quí' is cheer - ful, and filled with joy is

Em   **Am**   **B**

dor to - da la flo - res - ta. ¡Re - nue - va la crea -
liz. Can - ta en su a - la - ban - za: "co - quí, co - quí, co -
born, All the fields are ver - dant; cre - a - tion is re -
he, As he sings the prais - es: "Co - quí, co - quí, co -

Em   **A°7**   **B**

ción! Mi - ra el ro - jo li - rio; el duen - de ya bro -
quí." El pi - ti - rre can - ta y tri - na el rui - se -
newed. Look at the red lil - y; the 'duen - de' now has
quí." Mock - ing bird is chirp - ing, as is the night - in -

Note: "Coquí" is a small, frog-like creature that "sings." It is only found in Puerto Rico. "Duende" is a small purple flower.

Words & music: Pablo Fernández-Badillo, 1919 – , © 1977 Pablo Fernández-Badillo.
Used by permission.
⊕ English trans. Elsie Zala, 1925 –

tó. ¡Be - lla pri - ma - ve - ra que a-nun-cia su ful - gor!
ñor. ¡Cuán a - le-gre -men - te a - la - ban al Crea - dor!
bloomed: Beau - ti - ful the spring - time, its bril - liance show-ing forth.
gale, Sound-ing joy-ful an - thems, a sym - pho - ny of praise.

To - da flor sil - ves - tre, la ma - ya, el cun-dea - mor.
¡Có - mo se te a - la - ba en to - da la cre - a - ción!
Now all of the wild - flowers are sing-ing new songs of love,
How all of cre - a - tion re-flects the glo - ry of God!

¡To - do ma - ni - fies - ta la glo-ria de mi Dios!
All man - i - fest sure-ly the glo-ry of our God!

Yo qui-sie-ra ha - cer - lo en for-ma i-gual mi Dios.
I al - so would of - fer my songs in praise to God.

1066 O Brother Sun

1. O
2. O

Broth - er Sun,__ you bring__ us light,__ all shin - ing
Broth - er Fire,__ you warm__ our night__ with all____ your

'round__ in fier - y might. O__ Sis - ter Moon,__ you
danc - ing col - ored light. O__ Sis - ter Earth,__ you

heal__ and bless,__ your beau - ty shines____ in
feed__ all things,__ all birds,____ all crea-tures,__ all

Words: Adapted from St. Francis of Assisi, 1182 – 1226, by Sharon Anway, 1951 – ,
© 2004 Sharon Anway
Music: Traditional Scottish, adapted by Sharon Anway,
⊕ arr. Jason Shelton, 1972 –
YE BANKS AND BRAES, 8.8.8.8 D

C7   F   Dm7   B♭M7   Dm7

ten - der - ness. O— Broth - er Wind,— you sweep— the
scales—and wings. O— Sis - ter Death,— you meet us

B♭M7   Gm7   Am7   F/A E♭M7   F/E♭

hills,— your might - y breath— both fresh - ens and
here— and take— us to— our God— so

C sus4 C   Dm7   C/E   F

fills. O— Sis - ter Wa - ter, you cleanse— and
near. O— God of Life,— we give— you

Gm7 C7 Dm7   Gm7   C7sus4 B♭/C F

D.C. al Fine after verse 2

flow — through riv - ers and streams,— in ice— and snow.
praise— for all—your crea-tures,— for all— your ways.

1067 Mother Earth, Beloved Garden

1. Moth-er Earth, be-lov-ed gar - den, liv - ing trea - sure
2. Fa - ther Air, your in - spi - ra - tion holds to-geth - er
3. Broth-er Fi - re, great trans-form - er, share the pas - sion

un-der foot, All our days you ground our be - ing:
all that lives. As we breathe, our minds see clear - ly,
of the sun. In our hearths, your warmth re - vives us,

sage and this - tle, grass and root. Herbs to heal us,
lead - ing us to love and give. Rag - ing whirl-wind,
cooks our food and heats our homes. Flam - ing can - dle,

plants to feed us, land to till and tend and plow.
whis - pered breez - es, vio - lent gale and gen - tle cloud.
blood with - in us, blaz - ing des - ert, will to grow.

⊕ Words & music: Amanda Udis-Kessler, 1965 – , © 2004 Amanda Udis-Kessler

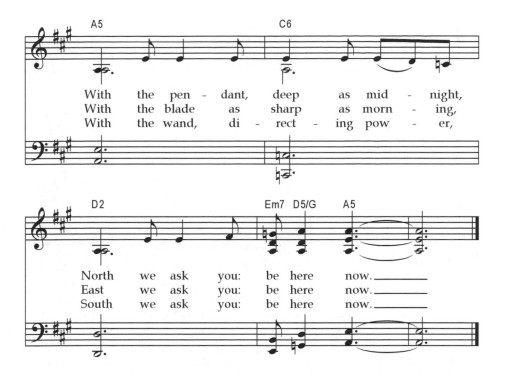

4. Sister Water, ever flowing, ocean, river, pond and rain.
   Drink we now and quench our thirsting; cleanse us, we begin again
   Mist and ice, a host of changes: all that courage will allow.
   With the cup, the holy chalice, West we ask you: be here now.

5. Lover Spirit, intuition in the center of our souls.
   In your love we find relation. All connected, we are whole.
   Timeless mystery, quiet conscience, deepest values, voice inside.
   With the drum and with the cauldron, this we ask you: be our guide.

1068   Rising Green

⊕Words & music: Carolyn McDade, 1935 – , © 1983 Carolyn McDade,
⊕arr. Jim Scott, 1946 –

stars____ for - ev - er have lain.____ 2. My____
love's____ e - ter - ni - ty.____ 3. I____
love____ blows o - ver the land.____ 4. My____
green____ to bring a new day.____

1069   **Ancient Mother**

♩ = **72** *(D Dorian)*

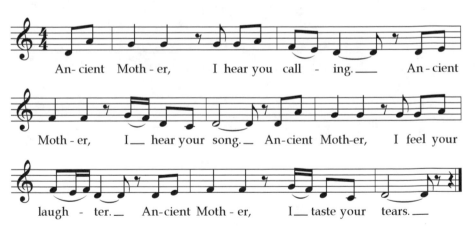

An - cient Moth - er, I hear you call - ing.__ An - cient

Moth - er, I__ hear your song.__ An - cient Moth-er, I feel your

laugh - ter.__ An-cient Moth - er, I__ taste your tears.__

Note: All of the Earth Chants, numbers 1069 - 1073, may be sung at the same time.

Words & music: Traditional Navajo prayer

Mother I Feel You

♩= 96 *(D Dorian)*

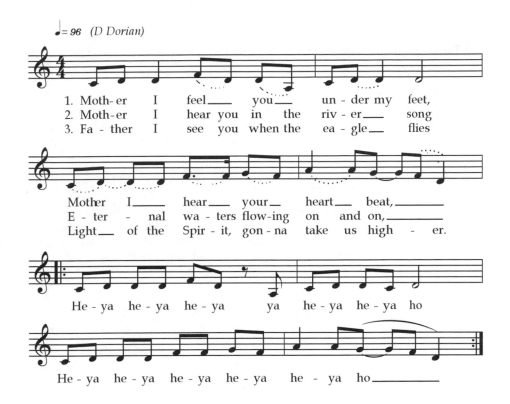

1. Moth- er   I   feel____ you____ un - der my feet,
2. Moth- er   I   hear you in the riv - er____ song
3. Fa - ther   I   see you when the ea - gle__ flies

Mother   I____ hear____ your__ heart__ beat,_____
E - ter - nal   wa - ters flow-ing on and on,_____
Light__ of the Spir - it, gon - na take us high - er.

He - ya he - ya he - ya   ya he - ya he - ya ho

He - ya he - ya he - ya he - ya he - ya ho_____

Words & music: Windsong Dianne Martin, 1954 – , © 1985 Windsong Dianne Martin

1071   On the Dusty Earth Drum

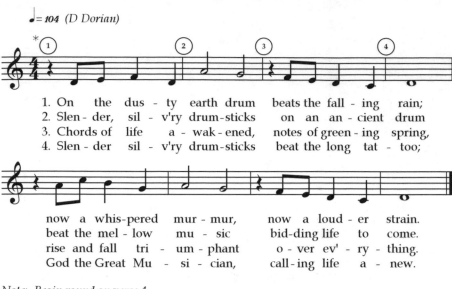

♩ = 104 *(D Dorian)*

1. On the dus - ty earth drum beats the fall - ing rain;
2. Slen - der, sil - v'ry drum-sticks on an an - cient drum
3. Chords of life a - wak-ened, notes of green - ing spring,
4. Slen - der sil - v'ry drum-sticks beat the long tat - too;

now a whis-pered mur - mur, now a loud - er strain.
beat the mel - low mu - sic bid-ding life to come.
rise and fall tri - um - phant o - ver ev' - ry - thing.
God the Great Mu - si - cian, call-ing life a - new.

Note: Begin round on verse 4.

Words: Joseph S. Cotter, Jr., 1895 – 1919
⊕Music: Jason Shelton, 1972 –
EARTH DRUM, 6.5.6.5

1072   Evening Breeze

♩ = 116 *(D Dorian)*

Eve - ning breeze, spir - it song,

sings to me when the day is done. Moth - er earth a -

wak - ens me with the heart beat of the — sea.

Words & music: Unknown, reprinted from *Circle of Song* © 1995
Full Circle Press, PO Box 32421, Santa Fe, NM 87594. All rights reserved. Used by permission.

The Earth Is Our Mother 1073

4. The Sky is our Father, we will take care of him. . .
5. The Sea is our Sister, we will take care of her. . .
6. The Forest is our Brother, we will take care of him. . .

Words & music: Native American, from *Songs for Earthlings*, ed. Julie Forest Middleton,
© 1998 Emerald Earth Publishing, Sebastopol, CA. Used by permission.

1074   Turn the World Around

1. We come from the fi - re, liv-ing in the fi - re,
2. We come from the wa - ter, liv-ing in the wa - ter,
3. We come from the moun-tain, liv-ing on the moun-tain,

go back to the fi - re, turn the world a-round.
go back to the wa - ter, turn the world a-round.
go back to the moun-tain, turn the world a-round.

Words & music: Harry Belafonte, 1927 - and Robert Freedman © 1975 Clara Music Publishing
Corp. (ASCAP).
Administered by Next Decade Entertainment, Inc. All rights reserved. Used by permission.
⊕ Arr. Jason Shelton, 1972 -

Whoa, _____ so is life! Ah, _____

so is life! Whoa, _____ so is life!

Ah, _____ so is life!

so is life! A-ba-tee-wah,_____ so is life!

Building in intensity - louder each time

D2

1. Wa - ter make the riv - er, riv-er wash the moun-tain
2. Heart is of the riv - er, bod-y is the moun-tain
3. We are of the spir-it, tru-ly of the spir - it

D2

Fi - re make the sun - light, turn the world a - round.
Spir-it is the sun - light, turn the world a - round.
On-ly can the spir - it turn the world a - round!

gliss. last time only

Whoa, _____ so is life! A-ba-tee-wah, _____ (ha!)

so is life! Whoa, _____ so is life! A-ba-tee-

wah, _____ (ha!) so is life! so is life!

Index of First Lines and Titles

(Titles are in capital letters)

Topical Index

WELCOME AND INGATHERING

Index of Composers, Arrangers, Authors and Translators